Partisans with a captured Pz.Kpfw.35 S 739 (f). The outlined turret number '313' indicates that it belonged to Panzer-Abteilung.202. In the background is an M3A3 light tank from the Partisan 1st Tank Brigade. We are not entirely sure what the circular objects hanging from the hull side are, although it is possible that they are elements of the roadwheels.

MRPC

The opposite side of the vehicle shown on the previous page shows that the tactical number was only applied on one side of the turret, and affords a good view of the German modified commander's cupola. The tank was captured near Trogir on 28 October 1944 and was subsequently used by the Partisan 1st Tank Brigade. The rearmost protective plate is missing from the suspension.

MRPC

A more complete view. The French and Italian 'Beutepanzers' of Pz.Abt.202 had stowage bins fitted over the back of the engine decks, this vehicle has one fitted to its rear wall, although the contents must have become rather hot with the exhaust so close. French tanks from 1940 (of which this is one) suffered from having no radio equipment so the Germans added their own, the antenna base for it can be seen on the hull side.

MRPC

Opposite: The Somua subsequently underwent a transformation from 'regular' Beutepanzer to something rather unique. During the winter of 1944-45, maintenance personnel at the Šibenik workshops went to considerable lengths to re-arm the tank with a 6-pounder gun from a wrecked AEC Mk II armoured car, which entailed extending the front of the turret. The tank is missing all of the upper protective plates for the running gear revealing the leaf spring suspension. Note the sheet metal strip at the bottom of the turret, perhaps a rain guard?

MNZS

Right: And here it is sometime later, in a ditch. Partisans are busy attaching tow cables in an attempt to flip it back onto its tracks. The right track has come off the drive sprocket.

V.Vuksic

Another Pz.Kpfw.35 S 739 (f) from Pz.Abt.202, this one the victim of a partisan anti-tank gun on a road near Prijedor in Bosnia on 27 November 1943. Like the Somua on the previous pages, it has a metal strip at the base of the turret, German modified commander's cupola and hooks on the glacis plate to hold spare tracks. Unlike the previous vehicle it has a tube protruding from the coaxial MG mantlet.

3x YHM

Looking at the opened hatches, it seems the partisans have had a good look around the tank. The left track has been broken and the curved armour plates are missing from the centre of the suspension, which is the most likely point of impact from the anti-tank round. The S35 was manufactured from large castings; two for the lower hull, joined longitudinally (the seam can be seen on the bow armour of this vehicle) and two for the upper hull, joined at the firewall. **YHM**

1, 2 & 3. A burnt-out Sd.Kfz.10/5 at Vukov Klanac, devoid of markings and licence plate.
4. Another Sd.Kfz.10/5 at Vukov Klanac, this one bearing a Luftwaffe licence plate and missing most of the 2cm Flak 38. Both vehicles have been back-fitted with the 'Behelfspanzerung' armour kit.
4x YHM

An unusual tracked vehicle to see in German service; an ex Belgian Vickers Utility Tractor, known as Artillerieschlepper VA 601 (b), shown here after a partisan ambush at Vukov Klanac in October 1944. It probably belonged to Pz.Jg.Abt.369 of 369.Infanterie-Division (kroat.). This Croatian division was employed against partisans in Croatia, Bosnia and Montenegro. The little schlepper had been towing a 7,5cm Pak 40, the shattered remains of which can be seen in front of the tractor. This is the version with folding sides (shown in the 'up' position) for the gun crew to ride in.

YHM

A pair of thoroughly destroyed Sturmgeschütz L6 mit 47/32 630 (i) at Vukov Klanac, probably from Pz.Jg.Abt.369 of 369.Infanterie-Division (kroat.). Both vehicles exhibit similar damage: a blown up fighting compartment, most likely the work of demolition charges. The vehicles carry the tactical numbers '221' and '222'. **MM**

A wider view of the Sturmgeschütz L6 mit 47/32 630 (i) on the previous page, where we can see that the entire front section has been blown into the foreground. The vehicle was right hand drive like the L6 and L3 tankettes and was designed for a two man crew, increasing to three, making for a very cramped fighting compartment. **YHM**

A destroyed column of ex-Italian Autoprotetto S37 APCs on the road between Imotski, Split and Sinj, Croatia in the Autumn of 1944. German forces seized 37 of these APCs after the Italian armistice and referred to them as Gepanzerter Mannschaftstransportwagen S 37 250 (i). They were issued to a number of infantry divisions and the 7.SS-Gebirgs-Division. These three have small armoured shields bolted to the top of the side armour and have their tyres reduced to ash.

MRN

A poorly exposed photo of an Autoprotetto S37 in partisan hands, this one in the Slovenian town of Ribnica after the Italian capitulation in 1943. The large size of the wheels is apparent in comparison to the partisans in the background. The S37 could reach 32mph on the road and had 8·5mm armour all round, with the exception of the floor which was 6mm.

MNZS

Slovenian partisans have destroyed an Autoprotetto FIAT 665, in German parlance a Gepanzerter Mannschaftstransportwagen Fiat 665 (i), most likely from a German Ordnungs Polizei unit or the Italian RSI Armoured Group San Giusto. These trucks were fitted with between 4 and 15mm of armour plate around the cab and on the upper part of the load bed. The 21 infantrymen in the back were supplied with 8 firing ports on each side and 3 at the rear. This vehicle has supports for a tilt, which may have kept the weather off those in the rear because there was no roof armour.

MM

A battered looking schwere Zugkraftwagen.12t (Sd.Kfz.8) driven by a Russian tanker rushes through downtown Belgrade on 19 October 1944. Barely visible on the rear of the vehicle is a standing white bear, the symbol of the 36th Guards Tank Brigade, the main Russian armoured unit engaged in the battle for Belgrade between 14 and 20 October 1944.

R.Marjanović

An RSO/01 with SS licence plate photographed at the Kalemegdan Fortress in Belgrade sometime after 20 October 1944. The vehicle appears to be missing its windows and the doors have dropped slightly, but other than that appears in good condition. The load bed has been modified with taller than usual sides and a replacement tilt frame. Folding chairs can be seen in front of and behind the RSO.

NSM

Partisans open the engine cover of an RSO/01 at Šent Jakob, Slovenia in May 1945. The RSO is missing its doors and driver's seat, but does have a full complement of 'snow shoes' on the side of the load bed. These provided extra 'flotation' on snow and were fitted to every third or fourth track link. As a result, the speed of an already slow vehicle had to be reduced yet further.

MM

A burnt-out RSO/01 in Yugoslavia and captured on film by a Bulgarian photographer. The frame of the driver's seat has tumbled out of the door and one of his steering levers is visible. The charring around the cab probably means that the engine caught fire

MPAB

Partisans pose with a blown up RSO/01. The force of an explosion has burst the cab rear wall and roof apart.

A.Smiljanic

Unexpected schlepper. Partisans of the 4th Vojvodjanska Brigade captured this schwerer Wehrmachtschlepper near Maribor, Slovenia, in May 1945.

NSM

Women walk through past the vehicles and heavy weapons of Kampfgruppe Stettner near the village of Boleč, southeast of Belgrade. The Kampfgruppe attempted to breakout through Belgrade to the north but lost these vehicles and weapons on 16 and 17 October 1944. The photos were taken by a Russian official photographer. **3x RGAKFD**

Panzer Zug Wrecks

A armoured train belonging to the Croatian 3rd Armoured Train Company captured in Kakanj, Bosnia, 30 March 1945. Partisans discovered three armoured trains consisting of 4 locomotives, 10 armoured wagons, 37 other wagons and one tank at Kakanj railway station. This one features characteristic Croatian-made armoured wagons with French APX-4 turrets from Somua S-35 or Char B1 bis tanks.

YHM

A Littorina Blindata Mod.42, German designation Eisenbahn Panzerbetriebwagen Littorina Mod.42 900 (i), photographed between Knin and Split, Croatia. Prior to the armistice in September 1943, the Italians employed 8 Littorinas in their '1. compagnia autonoma littorine blindate' in Yugoslavia. During 1944-45 the Germans used a further 7 Littorinas carrying the numbers 30 - 35 and 38, adding them to their armoured train force. This Mod.42 was armed with two 47mm guns in turrets, eight machineguns and an 81mm mortar. The 'V' shaped objects on the roof are supports for the (missing) frame antenna.
YHM

A Geschützwagen fitted with 10cm howitzer at the Central Tank Workshop in Mladenovac. The howitzer was an indirect fire weapon, so would be positioned near to the middle of the train, not at the end as shown here. To the left is a wagon for a 28cm Kanone 5 (Eisenbahn).
S.Rosić

Further along the train are a pair of Panzerjägerwagen. These were specially built incorporating turrets from Pz.Kpfw.IV, complete with 'Schürzen'. This turret is of the type fitted to a Pz.Kpfw.IV Ausf.J and has a swivelling commander's hatch, deleted gunner's vision port and no 'Nahverteidigungswaffe' on the roof. It also has a set of 'Schürzen' around the superstructure. These cars were supplied with an electric drive and were able to uncouple from the train remotely. The paint scheme appears to be a mix of factory and crew application.

S.Rosić

One of three captured schwere Spah Zug (numbers 202, 203 and 204) at the Central Tank Workshop in Mladenovac in 1946. In the foreground is a schwerer Schienen Pz.Artilleriewagen (artillery car) fitted with a Pz.Kpfw.III Ausf.N turret, behind it a schwerer Schienen Pz.Funkwagen (command car) with its frame antenna and behind that a schwerer Schienen Pz.Infanteriewagen (infantry car). The three dome-shaped objects on the front of the artillery car are ventilator covers for the engine. In the background is a lineup of captured Panzers, more of which we will see later.

S.Rosić

Partisans blew up the railway line between Virovitica and Našice on 16 April 1945 meaning that the crew of s.Sp.Zug.201 had to blow up their train at Čačinci station. Here we see a schwerer Schienen Pz.Funkwagen with its frame antenna partially destroyed.

NSM

Two Pz.Kpfw.M15 738 (i) tanks destroyed by partisans in the village of Belegiš on 8 October 1944. The photo on the left shows one of the less obvious modifications that Pz.Abt.202 made to their vehicles; sun shades over the driver's periscope and visor. Remains of the camouflage pattern seen on the rear of the leading tank.

3x NSM

Three Pz.Kpfw.M15 738 (i) tanks abandoned after a surprise German attack against Partisan lines on 3 and 17 January 1945 which pushed the partisans across the Srem plain. These tanks were discovered in the subsequent counter-attack which led to a stabilization of the lines until mid-April. The front view does not show the modifications seen on previous pages, ruling out Pz.Abt.202 as the user.

3x YHM

1 & 2. One of two Pz.Kpfw.M15 738 (i) tanks knocked out in Topčiderska Zvezda Square, Belgrade. During the fighting for Belgrade, Pz.Abt.202 reported that one of their M15s was rammed and flipped over by a Russian T-34. Could this be the tank? Notice the 'II' marking on the rear of the fighting compartment and the 'Jerrycan' rack on the engine deck.

2x A.Milosevic

3. Another of Pz.Abt.202s M15 tanks, tactical number '112' photographed at Šarengrad, Croatia, 15 February 1945. This one has a sheet metal strip at the base of the turret, like the Somua at the beginning of this book.

MM

A pair of Pz.Kpfw.M14 736 (i)s abandoned at the side of the road in Slovenia, May 1945. The tank in the foreground has shed its right track. Markings are simple; just a 'Balkenkreuz' on the side door.

MM

The victors and the vanquished. Russian soldiers look over an abandoned Pz.Kpfw.M15 738 (i) from Pz.Abt z.b.V.12 or 2./Pz.Abt.202 on a Belgrade street leading to the bridge over the river Sava. Just visible on the left is an Italian or French built truck and the rear of the Pz.Kpfw.L6 733 (i) seen on the next page.

R.Marjanović

Pz.Kpfw.L6 733 (i), tactical number '17' and Sturmgeschütz L6 mit 47/32 630 (i) both from Pz.Abt.z.b.V.12. Although a Panzer battalion, Pz.Abt z.b.V.12 had nine of these SP guns on its strength during this period. In the background is the Italian or French built truck shown on the previous page.

R.Marjanović

The Pz.Kpfw.L6 733 (i) clearly displaying its tactical number '17'. Although difficult to see, a white rhomboid, the symbol of an armoured unit, has been painted on the bow armour. Tanks such as this would prove no match for the modern and powerful AFVs fielded by the advancing Russians, its slow speed, thin armour and small gun making them unrealistic for anything other than anti-partisan warfare. With a crew of two men, the commander (who was also the gunner and loader) was overworked in combat. **NSM**

This Pz.Kpfw.L6 733 (i) was captured by partisans in the mountainous area of Gorski Kotar in Croatia, April 1945. It has large clear German 'Balkenkreuze', one making a good aiming point on the 30mm thick driver's front plate. The original Italian licence plate shows that the L6 was completed in late November 1941 and delivered to the Italian army in December. The object on the hull roof under the depressed gun, is the antenna base for the radio, which could pivot towards the rear of the tank when not in use.

MM

Photographed in Celje, Slovenia in May 1945 was this Sturmgeschütz L6 mit 47/32 630 (i). Markings consist of a simple black 'Balkenkreuz' and a German loading stencil on the side. The paint scheme appears to be brown or green patches over a 'Dunkelgelb' basecoat. As can be seen here, overhead protection was just a canvas cover than ran on guides fitted to either side of the fighting compartment.

MNZS

One push and it's gone. A Pz.Kpfw.L3 731 (i) abandoned in Kotor, Montenegro sits perilously close to the water's edge, the unusual style of 'Balkenkreuz' on the side is similar to those seen on L3s of 7.SS-Gebirgs-Division. It went on to serve with the Partisan 1st Bokeljska Brigade.

MM

Two Pz.Kpfw.L3 731(i) tankettes at an unidentified location in 1944. The vehicle in the foreground, which is missing its headlamps, looks as if the idler is damaged or the track has crept off. The L3 in the back of the truck has a 'Balkenkreuz' painted on the side. The L3 was designed to be transported in the back of a truck and, if needed, could dismount without a ramp.

YHM

Slovenia 1945. A Pz.Sp.Wg. AB 41 201 (i) has been captured by the Vojvodina Partisans. A tool box has been fitted to the back of the turret, a common addition in the Yugoslav theatre in 1945. Barely visible above the spare wheel is a 'Balkenkreuz'. The AB41 was powered by a SPA 88hp engine which gave the vehicle a top speed of 48mph.

NSM

The Pz.Sp.Wg. AB 41 201 (i) near Klagenfurt, Austria. The identifiers are the flattened front fender, camouflage pattern on the turret and 'Jerrycan' on the side of the engine bay. The upper section of the opened two piece door obscures the slogan on the side.

NSM

A unusual conversion of a Gepanzerter Munitionsschlepper UE 630 (f) photographed near Zagreb, Croatia at the beginning of May 1945. Someone, German or Yugoslav, has added an armoured superstructure which replaces the two dome-shaped covers for the crew. Here, the driver has limited vision - forwards only, while next to him, the gunner, has a machinegun mount from an Italian M13, 14 or 15 tank. The load bed at the back has been retained.

MM

A Bulgarian soldier stares at the bare carcass of a Pz.Kpfw.35R 731 (f) in Southern Serbia in October 1944. This tank was probably used as a donor to keep others in service, since everything of use (wheels, tracks, engine, interior) has vanished. The tank was most likely from Pz.Abt.z.b.V.12.

3x MPAB

Partisans file past a burnt out Pz.Kpfw.38 (t) in Slovenia, May 1945. In Yugoslavia these tanks were used on armoured trains and some would see Post War use. The large stowage bin on the trackguard is a field modification.

MM

Before: A Pz.Kpfw.III Ausf.N from Pz.Abt.212 retreating through the village of Buia (north of Udine, Italy) on 2 May 1945 with waving civilians. But all is not as it might appear. The foliage and blanket over the turret obscure its German markings and the commander is waving flowers. This was a ruse to fool the locals (and partisans) that the column was in fact the Allied liberators and was clearly successful. More information on this unit can be found in *Stefano Di Giusto's Panzer-Sicherungs-Kompanien and Panzer-Abteilung 208 - I./Panzer-Regiment Feldherrnhalle* by Tankograd Publishing.

S.Di Giusto

After: The tank from the previous page seemingly abandoned. Unfortunately the photo is of poor quality and was printed onto a textured paper, but nevertheless it is very unusual to find 'before and after' photos. **Inset:** Another of the Pz.Kpfw.IIIs passing through Buia, this one clearly displaying it's 'Balkenkreuz'. In fact this vehicle was shown on page 63 of Panzerwrecks 18, thanks once again to Stefano for spotting this. On the afternoon of 2 May, only hours after this photo was taken, Pz.Abt.212 was engaged in combat against C Squadron, 27th Lancers, in which they destroyed three Staghound armoured cars.

1x B.Dimitrijevic, 1x S.Di Giusto

Civilians look over an Alkett assembled Sturmgeschütz III Ausf.G, tactical number '131' near Slavija Square in Belgrade. The front view shows a shield shaped emblem painted onto the bow armour. The method of stowing spare roadwheels (two per side next to the engine air intake) is unique, as is the wooden frame around the engine deck, both being unit level modifications. We assume that the enormous stowage bin seen in the lower photo was kept on the engine deck and removed so the engine access hatches could be lifted.

1x R.Marjanović, 1x L.Archer

Above: A Sturmgeschütz III Ausf.G from the same unit as the one on the previous page. The identifiers are the unit insignia on the bow armour, method of attaching spare roadwheels and spare tracks in brackets above the roadwheels. It was abandoned on a roadside near Zemun, a district of Belgrade in late October 1944. **Right:** A Stug in action bearing each of the features highlighted above.

1x YHM, 1x NARA

October 1944, a partisan poses against the gun barrel of a Sturmgeschütz III Ausf.G, probably from Sturmgeschütz-Brigade.191 in Great Bečkerek, today known as Zrenjanin. This MIAG assembled vehicle has the number '307' painted on the 'Schürzen' and spare tracks over the front of the fighting compartment.

NSM

A wreck in the Kalmegdan Fortress, this one a MIAG assembled Sturmgeschütz III Ausf.G photographed in the spring of 1945 with its crew of Belgraders. The tactical number '5' doesn't give much away, and it could belong to SS-Stu.Gesch.Abt.1007, Stug.Bde.191, 202 or Kampfschule Niš, all of whom were in the area. Its tracks, along with the return rollers, have been removed. The welded hooks on the side and front of the fighting compartment would have carried spare track links.

L.Archer

A Sturmgeschütz M41 mit 75/18 850 (i) photographed after the fall of the Kalemegdan Fortress on 20 October 1944. The left track is missing, and no damage is visible to the running gear or trackguard, ruling out a mine strike. It is probable that it was abandoned and the track removed afterwards.

NSM

This Pz.Kpfw.M15 738 (i) photographed in Niš, Serbia was shown in Panzerwrecks 4 where we attribute it to Pz.Abt.z.b.V.12. This image was clearly taken after those in Panzerwrecks 4 because the tracks have been removed except for the bottom run, and the return rollers taken. What does the civilian population do with tank return rollers? A number in white is just visible on the bow armour.

YHM

5.(verstärkte) Polizei-Panzer-Kompanie

Yugoslav soldiers check out a Pz.Kpfw.T34 747(r) from 5.(verst.) Pol.Pz.Kp. The retrofitted German antenna base has been fitted with a 'Sternantenne' indicating that this was a command vehicle. The tank carries a tactical number '04' on the turret side, along with a simple outlined 'Balkenkreuz', a weathered 'Balkenkreuz' painted onto the glacis plate. In the background of the photo on the opposite page are two AEC Mk II armoured cars of the Yugoslav 1st Tank Brigade.

1x MNZS, 1x B.Dimitrijevic

5. (verstärkte) Polizei-Panzer-Kompanie

5.(verstärkte) Polizei-Panzer-Kompanie

Tank '07' abandoned at a crossroads near the German stronghold at Basovizza near Trieste. After fighting against the partisans on 29/30th April 1945, several tanks were destroyed or abandoned around this village. The partisans continued their advance into the city of Trieste the next day. The tank has been spray-painted in 'Olivgrün' and 'Rotbraun' over 'Dunkelgelb'.

AG Foto

A number of 5.(verst.) Pol.Pz.Kp's Pz.Kpfw.T34 747 (r) were destroyed or captured around Trieste near the end of the war. The example in this poor quality image is being inspected by partisans. Part of the two digit tactical number outlined in white, is visible behind the knees of the chap on the engine deck. It is possible that this is the same tank as seen on the previous page.

MNZS

5.(verstärkte) Polizei-Panzer-Kompanie

5.(verstärkte) Polizei-Panzer-Kompanie

Another wreck from the combat of 29/30th April 1945, destroyed on the Basovizza to Trieste road and photographed in May. It has been fitted with a German rubber antenna base on the hull side and 'Notek' headlamp on the glacis plate. Showing faintly on the turret side is a 'Balkenkreuz' and tactical number '02'. An explosion has unseated the turret.

1x MNZS, 1x 2TB

The opposite side of the vehicle shown on the previous page, but taken sometime later after the engine access panels have been removed and the left track broken. The tactical number and 'Balkenkreuz' are much clearer here. The 5.(verstärkte) Polizei-Panzer-Kompanie were equipped with 10 T-34s, all armed with the 7,62cm gun across two 'Züge'. The unit was deployed to the OZAK area in July 1944 and was present there until the end of the war.

MM

5.(verstärkte) Polizei-Panzer-Kompanie

5.(verstärkte) Polizei-Panzer-Kompanie

1. Tank '01' driving through the centre of Trieste in May 1945. This tank was shown on page 73 of Panzerwrecks 13.
YHM

2. & 3. Partisans pose with another captured T-34/76, with a mix of roadwheel types, in the area of Basovizza after the cessation of hostilities in May 1945.
2x D.Savic

A mystery Panther. Panthers were not officially issued to units Yugoslavia, but at least one, an Ausf.G, was discovered abandoned near a railway line in the Bačka/Vojvodina area and photographed in May 1945. The poor quality of the photo prevents us from spotting interesting details, but we can see that the tracks are missing and the driver's and radio operator's hatches have been jettisoned.

D.Savic

A surprise to see among the German, Italian and French AFVs is this Hungarian 40M Turán I, shown here with Vojvodina partisans in Senta, October 1944. There is no further evidence of its later use with the Yugoslavs.

A.Smiljanic

A Pz.Kpfw.IV Ausf.F from 13.(verstärkte) Polizei-Panzer-Kompanie photographed in Ljubljana on 21 May 1945 by Jakob Prešeren. The 'Balkenkreuz' on the smoke discharger has been blocked out and rudimentary red stars painted on each of the rear mudguards over the insignia of 13. (verst.) Pol.Pz.Kp., which is still partially visible. The roadwheel jack has been moved from its usual position on the trackguard to the rear plate. **Inset:** The insignia of 13. (verst.) Pol. Pz.Kp.

1x MNZS, 1x S.Di Giusto/F.Rodna

Jagdpanzer 38, tactical number '232' was captured by partisans of the 16th Vojvodjanska Division in the Baranya area during March 1945. This is the vehicle shown in Panzerwrecks 2 and has prominent red stars painted onto the glacis plate and side armour. The style of camouflage pattern defines this as a Škoda produced vehicle. It is probable that the vehicle belonged to Pz.Abt.202 who received 10 Jagdpanzer 38 in March 1945.

3x NSM, 1x YHM

With MP40s at the ready, partisans pose with a Jagdpanzer 38 in Celje, Slovenia. At first glance we thought this was '232' as seen on the previous page because it is from the same production batch, but the camouflage pattern so prevalent on '232' is not visible here. It has three 'kill rings' on the end of the gun barrel, a detail not often seen on the Jagdpanzer 38.

Muzej novejše zgodovine Celje, zbirka Josipa Pelikana, JP 6640-JPP193

Civilians seemingly go about their business while a Jagdpanzer 38 and Kubelwagen (in the background) sit abandoned on a Maribor street sometime between 8 and 15 May 1945. Maribor (Marburg in German) had the dubious distinction of being the most war damaged town in Yugoslavia.

A.Smiljanic

Initially we thought this was the same vehicle as seen on page 58, but close inspection shows that the camouflage, although very similar, differs. What looks like damage to the rear or roof armour is the opened engine cover and loader's hatch. The diminutive size of the child makes the Jagdpanzer look more impressive than it actually was.

NSM

An early production Jagdpanzer 38 behind a Sturmgeschütz M41 mit 75/18 850 (i) and in the background (visible underneath the Jagdpanzer) a second vehicle minus tracks. The clarity and size of the 'Balkenkreuze' on the M41 could mean that this is the same vehicle as shown on page 46. The Jagdpanzer went on to serve with the Yugoslav forces Post War.

NSM

1. A Pz.Kpfw.38 H 735 (f) has been blown onto its back, possibly by a large mine as the first suspension unit has been blown off and the track broken.

MM

2. The same vehicle photographed sometime later after the final drive had been removed.

MM

3. A partisan inspects a thoroughly destroyed Pz.Kpfw.38 H 735 (f). The stowage bin over the 'Hecksporn' indicates that the tank belonged to Pz.Abt.202. Note the early pattern idler and small arms scarring to the side of the engine compartment.

B.Dimitrijevic

Panzers in Post War Yugoslavia

1. & 2. Some of the captured Pz.Kpfw.IVs and Sturmgeschütze that were used for the creation of the Yugoslav 3rd Tank Brigade photographed at 'Trnje' barracks, Zagreb in the Summer of 1945. Here we see a MIAG assembled Sturmgeschütz (only a proportion of MIAG vehicles were fitted with the cast mantel), a Pz.Kpfw.IV 'kurz' and behind this a Pz.Kpfw.M15 738 (i).

2x NSM

3. Yugoslav crews maintain a Pz.Kpfw.IV Ausf.G in the summer of 1945, still in its German markings. The engine deck has been removed and part now sits on the trackguard. In the background is a Panther Ausf.A, another mystery Panther. Officially no Pz.Kpfw.IV 'lang' are known to have been used in Yugoslavia.

2TB

Six photos taken during a parade in Kragujevac on 1 May 1945, organised by the Partisan headquarters in Serbia. **1.** A m.Zgkw.8t (Sd.Kfz.7) towing a heavy howitzer. **2.** Two Panzerkampfwagen 35R 731 (f)s with two piece hatches replacing the original commander's cupola. **3 & 4.** A Pz.Kpfw.M15 738 (i) front and back. **5.** A Sturmgeschütz III Ausf.G. **5x YHM**

Another Sturmgeschütz III, and probably the last vehicle in the parade, as the crowds have gathered behind. All the vehicles had 'J.A.' (Jugoslovenska Armija - Yugoslav Army) painted on the front and rear and some exhibit small red stars, this Stug has them on the front of the fighting compartment, although this overexposed image makes them difficult to spot. This Stug was assembled by MIAG and built on a hull with 50+30mm armour on the bow, driver's side MP port and no 'Zimmerit.'

YHM

Panzers in Post War Yugoslavia

After the surrender of the Axis forces, the Yugoslav Army acquired a large number armoured vehicles. To date there is no documentary evidence on the numbers and types captured. Jagdpanzer 38 number '3' has the gunner, loader and commander getting a breath of fresh air as they are photographed at the Tenkovsko vojno učilište (Tank Military School) in 1947. Just next to the large '3' it carries the Yugoslav serial number '312'. It is unknown if the Yugoslavs replaced any of the external components making dating its production pointless. The vehicle has had its exhaust muffler removed (resulting in a loud noise) and has two of the three camouflage loops remaining on the hull side. Note how, with the loader's hatch open, the roof MG mount has to be rotated.

2x MCO

Panzers in Post War Yugoslavia

Following vehicle '3' is '5', complete with a replacement headlamp. About half a dozen or so Jagdpanzer 38s formed part of the tank battalion of the TVU at Bela Crkva, Serbia.

MCO

Vehicle '2'. This one is missing the exhaust muffler and the roof MG. In Yugoslav service the Jagdpanzer 38 was known as 'Ferdinand'. In the background are T34/85s, once an adversary of this tank destroyer.

MCO

Panzers in Post War Yugoslavia

These two shots show vehicle '1' kicking up the mud. This vehicle is something of a head scratcher because it has a hull with twin driver's periscopes and camouflage loops, but an old, heavy gun mantlet. The most likely explanation is that the mantlet has been replaced. The rear view on the opposite page shows the final pattern 8 holed ribbed idler wheel and once again a lack of exhaust muffler. Vehicle '5' can be seen in the background.

2x MCO

Captured Sd.Kfz.251s were used by Yugoslav forces until 1952/53 when they were replaced with US supplied vehicles. **Opposite page:** With heavy camouflage, a late production vehicle with flat visors used as a command vehicle of a T-34 tank brigade during manoeuvres held in Šumadija, Serbia in September 1949. **This page:** 'Korpus za narodnu odbranu Jugoslavije' (The Yugoslav People's Defence Corps) or KNOJ, had a single armoured company at its disposal. It was equipped with captured light armoured vehicles such as armoured cars and halftracks. The Sd.Kfz.251 (often referred to by the Yugoslavs as 'Hanomag') is shown on exercise near Belgrade in 1951. **2x MCO**

Panzers in Post War Yugoslavia

An AB41 armoured car, known in Yugoslav service as an SPA 5t, passes a Sd.Kfz.251/22 in the 1951 exercises. In German service the Pakwagen had a crew of 4, here it has a few more than that in the crew compartment and more still on the bonnet.

MCO

The AB41 seen on the previous page (it was the only one the unit possessed) has passed another Sd.Kfz.251/22. It, like the other vehicles shown in the series, belongs to KNOJ, who used German AFVs until 1952/53, when the batches of M8 Light Armored Cars and M3A1 Halftracks arrived as part of the US military aid programme.

MCO

Panzers in Post War Yugoslavia

Up close with the AB41. The object on the bow armour in front of the driver is the filler cap for the fuel tank in front of the driver. Details of this can be seen in Panzerwrecks 17, where the armour plate is missing. The spare wheels on either side of the AB series were free wheeling.

MCO

The commander of the AB41 appears to be consulting a map, and it is difficult to tell if the AB41 is moving or the m.SPWs. The machine gun crossing the frame is probably an 8mm Breda 37 fitted to a pintle on the back of one of the Pakwagens.

MCO

Panzers in Post War Yugoslavia

Two shots taken from the gunner's position of a Sd.Kfz.251/22. The AB41 now has the addition of infantry. **Opposite:** This image proves that the Yugoslavs operated at least three Sd.Kfz.251/22s Post War. With the camouflage materials draped over them it is difficult to discern details and colours, but the vehicle on the right appears to have a scruffy coat of whitewash.

2x MCO

Panzers in Post War Yugoslavia

Whereas the Pakwagen on the previous page was whitewashed (we think), this example, with one of its rear doors open, is in plain 'Russian green'. A soldier mans the rear machinegun.

MCO

A Yugoslav soldier makes an adjustment to a Drehkran (10t) auf Fahrgestell de s.Zgkw.18t (Sd.Kfz.9/2) belonging to the Central Tank Workshop at in Mladenovac, 1948. The garage in the background has at least three more Zgkw and a bus.

2x MCO

Panzers in Post War Yugoslavia

The Central Tank Workshop at Mladenovac was the main Yugoslav Army establishment for the collection, overhaul and repair of captured German AFVs. Here, in the courtyard of the workshop is a Drehkran (10t) auf Fahrgestell de s.Zgkw.18t (Sd.Kfz.9/2), probably the same example as shown on the previous page. The massive vehicle has its crane raised, counterweights deployed and has received a replacement front wheel and tyre. Next to it, a s.Zgkw.18t (Sd.Kfz.9) and Sd.Anh.116 trailer, perfect for hauling tanks. Further to the right is a British made trailer.

S.Rosić

Not the best quality photo, but it shows what a motley collection of German vehicles were present at the Mladenovac workshops in 1946. From left to right: Pz.Kpfw.I, 7,5cm Pak40/2 Sf. 'Marder II', 4,7cm Pak(t) (Sf.) auf Pz.Kpfw.I (Sd.Kfz.101), Pz.Kpfw.M15 738 (i), Pz.Kpfw.38 H (735) (f), Pz.Kpfw.L6 733 (i), Pz.Kpfw.35(t) and yet more Pz.Kpfw.L6 733 (i). Making an appearance in the right of the photo is a buffer from the Panzerdraisine shown on page 24.

S.Rosić

Panzers in Post War Yugoslavia

The Yugoslav 1st Tank Brigade was equipped with British AFVs (Stuart light tanks and AEC armoured cars), the 2nd, 3rd and 5th with Russian T34s. The 4th Tank Brigade was outfitted with captured German tanks and SP guns. Shown here in 1946 is a Pz.Kpfw.38 (t) Ausf.C als Zugfr.Wagen, referred to by the Yugoslavs as a 'Praga'. Most, if not all Pz.Kpfw.38 (t)s used in Yugoslavia were part of an armoured train, each BP-42 train possessing two. Note the triangular pennant on the front.

3x MCO

Panzers in Post War Yugoslavia

Two more shots of '554', both clearly showing the insignia of 'Komanda tenkovskih i motorizovanih jedinica' (Tank and Motorised Units Command); a silhouette of a tank against a white circular background. The location is the training ground near the Osijek barracks in 1946.
2x MCO

Panzers in Post War Yugoslavia

Panzers in Post War Yugoslavia

Opposite page: Tank '554' once more. In this view the red star on the plated-over machinegun aperture is visible. **This page:** Tank '555', a Pz.Kpfw.38 (t) Ausf.B als Zugfr. Wagen and still sporting its German camouflage pattern. The perforated box on the trackguard held tools, and this battered one has a tracktool sticking out. The suspension travel while traversing a ditch can be seen to good effect, with one of the roadwheels touching the upper track run.

2x MCO

Yugoslav mechanics working on the steering gear or brakes of Pz.Kpfw.38 (t) number '556'. Note how the circular plate in front of the radio operator has been removed.

MCO

Six mechanics hard at work in the engine bay of a MIAG assembled Sturmgeschütz III Ausf.G. Part of the 'Zimmerit' has been removed from the rear wall to accommodate a what looks like a Yugoslav flag. Under the waistcoated mechanic's elbow is the starter port, normally obscured by a pivoting armoured cover.

MCO

Tank and infantry training with a Pz.Kpfw.III Ausf.N at Osijek in 1947. Although foliage covers many interesting details, it is possible to see that the gun barrel is not fitted into its armoured mount and the hull sides have a neat 'Zimmerit' pattern. Documents show that the Yugoslavs named the Pz.Kpfw.III and IV according to the engine manufacturer: Maybach III and Maybach IV.

3x MCO

Panzers in Post War Yugoslavia

Two Sturmgeschütz III Ausf.Gs (known as 'Mark III') from the 4th Tank Brigade shown during infantry training in 1947. One has foliage on the barrel, the other has not. Both have cast mantlets and no visible 'Zimmerit'. The insignia of the KTMJ on the side is clear.

7x MCO

Panzers in Post War Yugoslavia

Another of 4th Tank Brigade's Panzers; a Pz.Kpfw.II bearing the number '451' and symbol of the KTMJ. The Yugoslavs referred to this tank type as 'Mark II', this one having been repainted in a single colour, probably a Russian green.

MCO

Yugoslavs pose with a captured mittlerer Schützenpanzerwagen (2cm) (Sd.Kfz.251/17), this one a late production vehicle with rear hinged engine cover. It is possible that this is the vehicle shown on pages 28 and 31 of Panzerwrecks 2.

2x SM

The military museum in Belgrade, 1947. A number of these AFVs survived and are now on display at the Kalemegdan Fortress, however some did not. The two photos above taken at the same location during an exhibition in 1951 celebrating the success of the partisans. Here the VK 1801 and Pz.Kpfw.M15 738 (i) have been pushed onto their sides.

5x MCO